Suffering In Comfort

How Owning Your Choices Will Set You Free

Denise Hansard

Suffering in Comfort
Copyright © 2014 by Denise Hansard

All rights reserved. No part of this book may be reproduced or transmitted in any form or by any means without written permission from the author.

ISBN (978-1-940170-41-1)

This book is dedicated to my family, and my best friend, my lover, my companion: Al. They all helped me to learn from my stories. Without everything that has happened in my life, I would not be here today to give my gift of transformation through my work.

Table of Contents

Introduction 7
Why 9
Become Aware 13
Understand the Impact 23
Take the Next Step 35
Step into Greatness 49
What Do You Do Now 59
Why Not? 63
Live Like You Were Meant To 71
R.O.A.R 73

Introduction

Congratulations! By choosing this book, you've taken the first step to **setting yourself free**! Way to go!

There is a reason you were drawn to this book. You understand, you feel, you *know* that this is your opportunity to go beyond your comfort zone and into something greater. Something *more*.

Everything good, fulfilling, and important in life begins with noticing the opportunities...but only a few are willing to reach for them, to act upon them, to *make the choice to live free* and reap the benefits of those opportunities! The fact that you're here *reading this book* tells me that you're one of those amazing people!

I took my own journey of growth and healing with many steps forward and many more steps backward. You have chosen differently! By allowing me on this journey with you, I am honored and humbled to help you avoid the pitfalls and traps that slowed my growth, delayed my healing. Thank you!

This book is just the beginning of your own transformation, your own journey to the life you were meant to live! I want to offer you more wonderful gifts that you can receive on my website www.denisehansard.com

I know that the exercises in this book are only the first step on your journey, and because **you**, where so many others choose to continue *suffering in comfort,* **you** have taken that first step, I am offering a special gift to you.

Visit me at www.denisehansard.com/go/firststep and receive a complimentary Exhausted to Exhilarated Discovery Session. We'll speak together by phone, and talk about where you are, where you *want to be,* and I'll help you map your potential next step! I'm not in the forest with you – I can see the trees, and it has been my pleasure helping so many others just like you find their map to the greatness they always knew was within!

Remember, One Choice Can Change YOU! What *choice* will you make *today*?

I can't wait to speak with you!

Why?

"Don't cry because it's over, smile because it happened." -Dr. Seuss

No one told me, but somehow I knew—he was dead. And the voice in my head was screaming, "He killed himself!" I remember saying just those words to a friend that morning. In that moment, I was struggling to make a decision, to choose the "right" thing to do. Do I go at lunch to find his body, or do I wait until after work?

This was a defining moment for me. Instinctively I knew my lover, my best friend, my companion had taken his life: just as I knew that the sun was shining bright on that cool March day. Deciding on the time to find his body was the first of many choices I had to make in my new life without him.

We all have our stories—it is about how we *own* the choices in those stories that matter.

You might think this book is about suicide—but it's not. Suicide is just the event that happened to me. It's an event much like any other that may have happened to you—whether it's divorce, job loss, a promotion, an award won, or even the birth of a child. Suddenly, you have important choices to make. Choices on what happens next in your "story." Our choices—big (like mine that day) and small—

define us. What kind of life story we have is all about how we *own* the choices we make.

Yes, that day changed me forever. It was during this time of grief, of feeling that I had been rejected and left because I was not good enough to keep my lover alive, that I became aware of what was really happening. My thoughts—and my feelings around these thoughts—would determine my choices.

There would have been a certain comfort in choosing to die with him. That could have taken the form of my own suicide, which I seriously considered. Or living into the story of "the woman whose lover killed himself"—an object of pity and one from whom no one expected too much. *(I did choose this one for a while)*. Or the best choice for me at the time: to take back control of my thoughts and begin to live again. You can guess which one I chose.

I'm betting that you picked up this book because you understand what I am talking about ... that our choices define us, our choices determine who we become. This awareness of our choices gives us an opportunity. It allows us to become more than we ever thought we could be—our "best self." Or we can choose to stay stuck in our suffering, in our past stories of regret, loss, lack or unworthiness—whatever that may be for you.

Imagine for a moment that you could be that famous *phoenix* rising out of the ashes to live again. To choose thoughts that empower you instead of the negative ones you have had in the past. To see the impact that your thoughts have on how you behave—and change this to better support you. To know the process of what to do next.

Our choices define us, our choices determine who we become.

That is what this book will do for you: give you the four simple steps to making—and owning—your choices:

Become aware
Understand the impact
Take the next step
Step into greatness

This is how you don't let your **BUTS** stop you!

That is what I want for you: to be able to live the life you were meant to, and not be controlled by your emotions and your self-deprecating thoughts. Or, more importantly, by your past, your history—the story that you have chosen to determine your life. Until now.

There is a quote hanging in my office that I choose to live by every day: "It is not what happens to you, but what you do with what happens to you that matters."

Let me help you to make your life matter—to you and to everyone around you.

Taking the steps needed to move forward toward a new you are the reason for this book. If you do the work, then it will work for you.

> *"There is no greater agony than bearing an untold story inside you."* -Maya Angelou

Become Aware

*"The mind is everything.
What you think, you become."* -Buddha

Become Aware – Open Up to Your Story

Open up to your story so that you can really see where you are *today*! Knowing this will allow you to work on that new story for *tomorrow*.

We all have our story. Becoming aware of it is the first step. Then you can determine how this story will work *for* and not against you.

When people ask who you are, what do you tell them? And is what you tell them really *true*?

Do you know that there is only 5% truth in any story that we tell? The other 95% is what we have *chosen to believe* as our story: the history that we allow to become our life. We forget the real truth that happened to us. Or we choose to see ourselves as the hero, the victim, or someone who needs to be rescued. We stay stuck in the comfort of our pain, sometimes suffering in silence.

Stories *Not* Worth Sticking To

We become committed to stories with a sense of lack. This is important! How much time do you spend thinking of yourself as not being loved, never having enough love, being a person who is not good enough or pretty enough, or being the outcast in a group of people—always feeling invisible? Or, when you think of money, you consider yourself as not being good enough to have much money: it is just not meant to be yours. You have lived so long in the story of not having money that you can't seem to get it. And—no matter how hard you try—you always need more. No matter how hard you try for that promotion within the company, you are just not good enough to be the selected one, not good enough to be worthy of the additional financial freedom it would give you. Just not good enough, period!

This is also true for any *job* that we do. You tell yourself that you just need to choose something that will make a good living and stick with it, no matter how much you may hate it. That's just how life is. Staying in the J.O.B—just over broke—is what is meant for us. This way of thinking keeps us embedded in the victimhood of our stories—so much so that we have become powerless.

Yes, there is some truth to any and all stories. It's just that this truth is only a small part of who we are. The rest is what keeps you stuck, keeps you small, and keeps you in fear. You're unable to move out of your comfort zone, out of your suffering in the comfort of your pain. I can tell you staying stuck in the comfort of your pain can *kill* you.

Here's how I know.

My Story

I grew up in the South. My parents survived the Great Depression and held tightly to the mentality that went with it. You know what I'm talking about. There would never be enough of anything: food, money and—most definitely—love. The lessons they instilled in me and their other three children were "work hard and you might amount to something," and "you have to realize that whatever you do has consequences."

Then there were the personal messages I received, from my grandmother, no less. It was the summer I was eight years old. Georgia summers were hot and humid. My shorts and t-shirt were sticking to me, as the air was not moving at all. We had been playing and were just ready to go inside to rest when my grandparents drove up in their truck. We knew we had to suddenly become presentable for them. This was just the way you did things in the South. So, my sisters and I lined up in front of my grandmother. We stood there, longing for some kind words, some sign that we were "enough" to receive her love. She said nothing. Not a word did she say to any of us ... until she got to me.

It was then that I heard those words that would forever haunt me—that started and continue to reinforce my sense of unworthiness.

"If you would only lose weight, people would like you more. No wonder you don't have many friends."

This story—combined with all of the other stories that made me feel "less than," especially from the people who were supposed to love me, like my grandmother—left me feeling I would never be good enough, no matter what I did. I would never be thin enough or pretty enough. So I should just do what everyone else was doing and try not to stand out—and call attention to all I lacked. Don't take risks or the "consequences" will haunt you forever. "Pain, pain, suffer, suffer" became my mantra.

What has been your comfort zone of suffering, your mantra in your life.

I've struggled with feeling as though I'm unworthy for most of my life. I did step out of my comfort zone and do some risky things: like continue to change jobs and companies in a family where you were supposed to stick with one employer for your entire career. I was the one that couldn't stay in one place for too long. I would embark on these career changes as my own personal adventures. My family would quickly point these out as mistakes and misdeeds, and not be loving and supportive the way I wanted. I was told I could do anything, and yet discouraged to take risks. Mixed messages abounded. They would offer support, yet at the same time shake their heads and lament, "Here she goes again with those harebrained ideas." Does this sound familiar? Did you experience your own version of "pain, pain, suffer, suffer"?

As I grew, I chafed between those two poles: my sense of unworthiness on one side, and my sense of wanting to be "me" on the other—the risk taker, which made me in my mind the black sheep of my family. It was not until I was in my late twenties, involved with a wonderful man (not acceptable to most of my family, as he was African American and I was a lily white Southern girl) that I began to really spread my wings and start to see new possibilities. Al and I grew with each other. We loved learning and investigating ideas, such as how the mind affects our health and our emotions, along with how to really begin getting what we wanted in life. We were on a path toward enlightenment and empowerment.

Then came that devastating day when Al killed himself. I didn't just lose him: I lost me. I lost who I was without him in my life. For nearly nine years, we had been together, as one. Al and I worked together, played together and loved together. Did we go through our difficult times? Of course. Did we work through those difficulties? Yes. Those times just made us stronger.

I ached with the loss of him, our intimacy, our friendship, our future—until I just wanted the ache to go away. One evening months after his death, I had made my decision—I was going to kill myself, too. I just couldn't see past the darkness of my life without him in it. The ache, the pain of being left behind, was just too great to take.

Having a very analytical mind, I made clear plans about the "how" of my death. I did not want it to be messy, as I was not a messy person. I wanted just to not *feel* any more. So pills and alcohol were the way for me. I gathered everything I needed and set about doing "it" right.

I remember having the pills in one hand with the bottle of Tequila near. When I was just about to swallow that handful of pills, I heard a voice in my head. It was as clear as if a person I loved were standing right next to me, speaking directly in my ear. "How will your family feel if you do this?" This was a voice I knew. You can call it divine intervention or whatever resonates with you. I listened to this voice, as I had heard it before. At that moment, I just couldn't do it. I crumbled to the floor, curled into a ball, and cried as if my very life depended on it. And it did. I had made a choice: the choice to live.

Knowing some of what was happening in Al's life at that time, it was clear to me why he made the choice that *he* did. He believed his pain was too great to live with. The "good girl" in me understood his "why." This was my way of trying to avoid judgment and be compassionate. The "abandoned girl"—the one he rejected and over whom he chose death instead—was angry, sad, and devastated. Intellectualizing versus pain. These were conflicting emotions. I was quickly taken back to my sense of not being enough, of not being worthy. I mean, come on, if I was "enough," then he would still be here, right? That was my thinking, even though I had made the choice not to die with him. "Pain, pain, suffer, suffer."

So I muddled through life, living outside of myself for a long time. I gained weight: about 20 pounds on a 5'2" body, which was not thin to begin with. So my inner negative voice told me that I was not a pretty sight. I put on weight because I didn't want anyone to look at me and see my pain: I wanted to be invisible! "Dowdy" was the word for me. This was the only thing that fit my self-image, since it seemed I wasn't good enough for anyone. Most importantly, the person I thought loved me the most had left me behind!

Even if you have not experienced losing a loved one to suicide, I am sure you have had moments of a vast loss. The departure of a job that took your identity with it. The divorce you believed could have been prevented "if only you had been good enough." The bankruptcy that told the world you were a failure! The list of stories of lack goes on and on.

This became my story for a long time: being a victim to suicide. My family didn't know what to do, so they just stayed away and didn't deal with me. I put on a good face for them, because I didn't want them to know how much pain I was in. I know you may have felt the same way—just keep moving, and hold everything inside because no one understands you. No one really wants to see you in pain, since it reminds them of their own pain. If our loved ones are in pain, how can they help us? So we stay stuck in the comfort of our pain!

Whether or not it was the truth, this was how I felt. My story was being the victim of suicide: of the girl who lost a loved one to a suicidal act. It wasn't until I made a choice to define my story and begin to own the choices I had made in my life so far, that I was able to live more freely without suffering in the comfort of my pain.

What's *Your* Story?

Telling your story—literally writing it out—is the beginning of your transformation. To begin making any change in our lives, we must first know that we *have* to change, along with owning that we *want* to change.

How do you do that? Start by telling all about yourself: as if you are writing a book, which will become a movie of your life. In your mind and heart, you have been taking notes on your life. You have been living through those notes without ever really knowing what they were.

What will your story be? By identifying and writing it, you become aware. You open yourself up to becoming more: to becoming more of who you were meant to be all this time.

Not all stories are as devastating as mine. But now is *not* the time to think, "She had it much worse than *I* did." That's just another way to stay stuck and never change. This is not a contest to see who has the saddest story. It really doesn't matter, as our story is "our story"—the one that defines us and, if allowed, keeps us stuck. Just get your story out there, so you can start looking at it to see why you are where you are today.

Step 1: Become Aware Through Your Story

Here's how to begin.

Write your story as if you are telling it directly to me, as your friend who can help. Tell me all about your childhood, your teen years, your life up to now. Focus on the events that seem to stay in the forefront of your mind, causing you pain or sorrow or angst. It could be about your relationships, your schooling, and your career—even about your pets, if that left a lasting impression on you. Tell me what your parents taught you about money, love, working, relationships, etc. I want to hear it all.

Why is this important? Telling our story gives us an awareness of who we are and, most importantly, the "why" of us. Most of us want to grow beyond where we are today. We want to have it all: more money without the fear of losing it all, a loving relationship without any sense of not being good enough, and a career that inspires us to be who we are, and not feel as if we are an "outcast" within our groups.

To have all that, we must be able to pull back the curtain and look deeply into our souls. You may have forgotten who you really are inside. That often happens when you have not been supported to be more. Looking into the stories that define who you are today will unlock greater potential for being *more* in your life for the present and the future. For being a more *"real"* you—the "*YOU*" you have always wanted to be.

The *Rest* of My Story

I almost killed myself because I was so stuck in my grief, my story of being left alone, of being abandoned. There seemed to be no one to help me get out of it. I was holding the pills in one hand and a bottle of tequila in the other. I wanted the pain to end, and I knew this was the way to take care of that. Along with this was the thought that I would be with Al again. That's when the voice asked, "How will your family feel if you do this?"

In that moment, I knew I couldn't do to *them* what had been done to *me*. I eventually sought out help and started putting my life back together. I did the work that saved me. And I learned so much about the process that I realized it's my calling to share it with you.

You probably know about Stephen King: the most wonderful horror storyteller in the world (or at least in mine). What you may not know is a story that took place later in his life. In 1999, he began to write about his craft of writing: through stories about his life. One day in the middle of that process, he was walking along the road to his home. He was hit by a car and almost died. A man who wrote about things that could scare us to death suddenly was fighting for his life. It took him months to recover. During that time, his stories became his path to recuperation.

He tells about this in his book *Stephen King: A Memoir of the Craft On Writing*. If you haven't read it, do!

Writing is a process. It will begin to help you to heal, to make you whole, to put you into the right frame of mind to move forward.

Here's what I want you to do. Let's set a goal together. By doing this work, you will have a "story" to tell that no longer defines you by the limits it sets on your life—but is about the wonderful experiences you invite into it. To begin to live the life you were meant to live.

"Become alert to what passes your mind." -Unknown

Become Aware Action Work

Purchase a journal for this work, and this work alone. Write your name and date on the inside. You will appreciate this when you have completed the work and can go back to see how far you have come.

Write your *story*!

Schedule time to begin. Just write. Don't let anything stop you! No critiquing, no criticizing ... Just write as if your live depended on this. It does.

You will find writing is quite cathartic. It allows you to become aware of thoughts about your past, your present and your future.

It is in these thoughts that the process to changing your story—truly getting a "do-over"—will begin to take shape.

Homework for right at this moment: WRITE IT DOWN!

Not sure where to begin? Here are some questions that may help you:

1. If you could change anything in the way that you were raised, what would it be?
2. What is your first clear memory of feeling "sad" or "rejected" or "not good enough"? Describe that time and what was going through your mind.
3. What story stands out in your childhood? Tell me about it in detail. Paint a picture so I can see it too.
4. Do you feel an emptiness inside that you can't seem to fill? Do you use food, drugs, alcohol or something else as a means to fill it? When did this practice start? When you use this method to get "full," what is going on in your head?

5. What has happened recently that caused you to question yourself and what you are doing in your life?

6. What stories did your parents tell you about you? About themselves? About your grandparents? These stories define our foundation of being. Knowing these stories helps us change and shift our perceptions.

Nothing that you write in your journal needs to be shared with anyone else—unless you want it to be. This is yours and yours alone! The process of just getting it out is the beginning: the start to your becoming aware and to transforming your life. Don't judge your story. All our memories become our stories—which define us, because we made choices based on those memories.

Remember: only 5% of what we tell ourselves through our stories is the truth. The rest is just our perception of what happened. Let's begin now to change your perception and change your life.

It is your perception of what happened in your life that defines you. Own the choice to change it.

Understand the Impact

> *"Man is a thinking center, and can originate thought. All the forms that man fashions with his hands must first exist in his thought; he cannot shape a thing until he has thought that thing."*
>
> Wallace Wattles, The Science of Getting Rich

Understand the Impact – Your Thoughts Create Your Life

Wallace Wattles tells us that everything is created twice: first in your thoughts and then by your actions. This is the key: understanding that our thoughts create the events, the situations and the feelings of what happens to us.

Finding within yourself the means to really understand what has happened so far in your life is *transformation*. You no longer have a need for blaming, criticizing, or condemning yourself or others.

When you are able to nourish your present life, and how you became who you are today, you can release the negative emotions you have been harboring. Being able to love *you*—and let go of persistent thoughts of "not being good enough," "not having enough," "I had a tough life" or even that "life growing up was dangerous"—will have a profound effect on how you live the rest of your life.

Most of us feel we had hardships—things we had to endure in our past. You have identified these by telling your story. That's why it is important to write your story. You need to understand how your thoughts created your story. Realizing that *our choices shape our story*, we can see we have the ability to change that story.

Going through the healing process after Al's death, I realized that I had a choice. I could either stay in the comfort of my pain, or I could move beyond it to a new life without Al. This was quite a process! It began with me realizing that my thoughts created my reality. I had a choice to be depressed and unhappy, lost and alone. I had a choice to think I was "ugly" and "dowdy." I had a choice to determine how I would be in the career world without him by my side. I had a choice to change my thoughts about me, and the impact of these thoughts on who I was to become.

Wow: what a powerful idea! I could begin to think the thoughts that would help me to heal! Suffer, suffer, pain, pain was *not* inevitable! I didn't need to feel out of control in my life. I could *choose* my thoughts—and choose to have a better life.

How many times have you felt your life was swirling out of control? And when this happened, did you *see* that you created this feeling?

"I Don't Need Help"

For me, the sense of being in harmony with my life didn't happen overnight, and it didn't happen alone. First, I denied that I even needed help. I mean, come on, I was a counselor and could heal myself! Not surprisingly, that didn't work. So I sought out self-help books, researched professional journals, and eventually got the structured professional help that I needed. Yes, I got into therapy when I felt ready for it, which—some of my friends thought was almost too late.

I look back now and can see the impact of those choices. At first, I didn't make a conscious choice to heal. I was in denial that I needed any help. Thank goodness for my friends! They saw what I needed more than I was willing to choose for myself.

My best friend, Linda, was the first one to help me to understand that I had a choice: getting help or suffering in my pain. She saw what was going on and that I was not healing. I would wake up each day at 3:00 a.m., sobbing, weeping, lamenting my loss. I would pull myself together enough to get ready for work and put in my eight hours. The moment I got in the car to drive home, I began to cry again. I was spiraling down that rabbit hole ... heading toward emotional destruction.

I often talked to Linda about my pain and the spiraling effect, yet did nothing to move beyond this. It is so much easier just to talk about how "bad" our lives are, how we have it so much worse than others, that this becomes our identity. Pain, pain, suffer, suffer.

Little did I know that Linda was my guardian angel. She reached out to a psychologist friend of ours, Phil, hoping that he would be able to get through to me when she could not. When Phil called to talk with me, using his ever so "soft voice of understanding," I was pissed! I didn't need his help! All I needed was to be in pain, to be the martyr of loss, to be the "suicide survivor."

Are you choosing to "spiral" in the pain of your story?

This voice of denial was a way for me to stay stuck in my suffering, in my comfort of pain. Also, this was the grief working its way out, but I couldn't see that. It wasn't until this phone call that I began to realize how much I was suffering ... and how comfortable

I was there. I was choosing to keep this going until someone called me on my "stuck-ness" and my willingness to stay there.

"Pissed" & Embarrassed

Being "pissed" was just the beginning. I was also embarrassed. You know what I mean. Being the so-called "healer," I was unable to help myself. You might have this embarrassment due to losing a job or filing for divorce or, even still, declaring bankruptcy. All of these events can be embarrassing and can be seen as something of a failure in other people's eyes.

My reasoning was that I didn't want anyone to know how much pain I was in. This was another defining moment for me. My choice before of being "stuck in pain" was no longer what I wanted. It became clear that I had to make the choice to move past my comfort zone of suffering. And the place to begin was with understanding the impact of my choice to stay in grief and pain.

What has been one of your defining moments? Or are you still in the comfort zone of suffering? Are you allowing your thoughts to keep you stuck in the comfort of your pain? What thoughts are you having about those hardships of yours: having lost the job that gave you your identity as a provider? Going through a divorce that robbed you of your identity as part of a couple? Declaring that you are a financial failure? Feeling you are not good enough for the life you are even afraid to want?

Here's what I have discovered—a formula for life.

Thoughts = Feelings = Actions = Results

Our thoughts create our feelings. Our feelings create our actions. Our actions create our results. And then it begins all over again. Most of us get as far as this: if we aren't happy with our results, we change our actions. This places us in a vicious cycle of changing our actions, not realizing that we need to go back to the impetus—which is our *thoughts*. If we want different results, we change our thoughts. It is that simple.

Napoleon Hill states it this way in his book *Think and Grow Rich*:

> *Our minds become magnetized with the dominating thoughts we hold in our minds and these magnets attract to us the forces, the people, the circumstances of life, which harmonize with the nature of our dominating thoughts.*

Simple plan—change your thoughts if you want different results.

"Change my thoughts, change my life." Sounds good, right? But is it doable? I get that's what you could be thinking right now—because that's what *I* thought when I first heard this. "Really?! If it was as easy as this, why isn't everybody doing it? And why did it take me so long to get it?"

And it *did* take me years to finally put this into practice. That is the reason I am sharing it with you. I don't want you to spend years stuck in your pain—thinking that it's all you deserve, so you may as well get comfortable with it. To not grow beyond the pain into all the wonder and joy there is in store for you. I want you to start today with this four-step process to begin to live like you were meant to.

The Seductive Ego

Before we get into the action steps for this part, let's look at one more thing ... our ego. Why? For one very simple reason: we all have an ego and probably don't truly understand how it affects us.

Here is how I view "ego": that part of our being that creates our sense of self; our sense of worth or self-esteem; our sense of importance to our life. In the psychoanalytical world, it is "the part of the mind that mediates between the conscious and the unconscious and is responsible for reality testing and a sense of personal identity." To me, this really means the ego is the reasoning portion of our mind that will help to determine our value in any given moment.

As you can see, the ego is there to protect us. However, it does not always serve us in an empowering way. Did you know the ego has six needs? Or as published in a "Psychology Today" article by Gregg Henrique, these are the six elements of ego functioning:

1. The degree of incite (awareness)
2. The degree of agency and self directedness (ability to control and guide environment/circumstances)
3. The degree of self-esteem, acceptance, and compassion (respect and value)
4. The degree of empathy with others (relationship to others)
5. The degree of integration, purpose, and thematic coherence (desire to engage socially)
6. The degree of philosophical and moral development (point of view; sense of direction toward self)

(If you want to know more, look up his article in *Psychology Today*, June 27, 2013 issue.)

Right now, let's address how our ego can hold us back from understanding the impact of our thoughts and how we can change them. Our ego—our mind, our thoughts—is a curious creature. It always wants to know more. So it seeks to question all that we do, all that we hear, and all that we think.

That would be great if it would just stop there. But, no, it goes further into *analyzing* everything that it's curious about—it goes into reasoning mode. This starts up that voice inside of all of us that makes statements like this:

"What makes you think you can do **that**?"

"You have tried time and time again to lose weight. Why do you think you can do it **now**?"

"You **know** that's the best you will ever be"

Or, one of my favorites:

"You'll **never** make any money by jumping from job to job. Stick with one company and get a pension: a retirement plan. That's the way to go. Otherwise, be willing to suffer the **consequences**."

We think of this as "the voice of reasoning"—in part, because that's what your ego *wants* you to call it. But I like to label it the "seductress." This is the ego trying to protect us. It seduces us in to thinking that we will be safe by staying right where we are, doing the same things that we have always done, and still getting the same results. Is this true for you?

Pop Goes the Ego!

Do you notice when your ego pops up for you? Doesn't it feel as though it is trying to seduce you into not moving forward into something new? This is why I call it the seductress. It calmly enters our mind. It is a constant companion talking to us … we don't know it has a hold of us until it is too late! We have been seduced into a state of fear, fatigue, confusion—keeping us stuck. Again, suffering in comfort just by not "dealing" with the pain can be the easiest route to take. This inner voice, in our current way of thinking, says things that sound as though they are true, and that is exactly what we should do.

After years of grieving and healing, I finally understood that my voice of reason was not doing me any good. I was tired of being in pain. Tired of that voice telling me to stay where I was, since I was not good enough and staying in my grief was safe. I couldn't be hurt by someone else if I stayed there, in my "pain, pain, suffer, suffer."

Choosing to Think

Then I started making different choices. It wasn't as if I just woke up one day and decided to do this. It was moments in these days over weeks, over months and, yes, over years. I would have those times when I felt as if I would die if I didn't make a different choice in my life, and then I would crawl right back in my comfort zone to continue the same way that I had been before.

I know this pattern is not mine and mine alone. This is the way we are wired. Do what it takes to stay protected, to stay suffering in our comfort zone. Remember the ego? It is only when our spirit breaks free from our limited mind that we begin to move beyond the "curtain of fog" that has been holding us back. It is then that we start taking four steps forward—with only a *small* step back—until we are finally taking more steps away from the pattern that made up our lives until now. Then we make a choice, a more empowered choice, and begin to run toward a new life and new choices.

I was ready for that way of life, the *formula* that people had been giving me and pushing me to try. I started paying attention to my thoughts—actually "defining" them. Next, I became more aware of my feelings, my actions and, ultimately, my results.

One way I did this was through journaling. I wrote every day and have journals upon journals with my thoughts, and behaviors. Doing this gave me the chance to begin identifying what I was feeling. That led me to begin to question my "seductress," to decide if what my ego was telling me was or was not true. I began to notice

Choose positive thoughts even in the midst of negative circumstances.

what was happening to me through my pattern of thoughts.

I began to choose more positive thoughts. Even if I didn't *believe* them, I *thought* them. The hardest thing to do is be aware of our thoughts and choose *positive* ones. I kept doing this until, one day, the positive thoughts came on their own! Then my feelings began to change. I started feeling more alive and having more energy every day. This energy scared me at first! I had been pretty dead inside, just occasionally peeking out of the deadness, seeing the "me I used to be." I started training my mind to notice my thoughts, pause long enough to decide what to do, and then do *that*—with *that* being a defined way of living.

With more defined thoughts and feelings, my *actions* started changing. I walked with my head high. No longer did I need to look down or away when I approached people—because I didn't *want* to be invisible anymore. I laughed more and found people laughing with me. I recognized that the results of my life were different: they were more of what I used to be before the suicide. I remembered that person. It was like coming "home." Most importantly, I remembered loving that person.

Let's look at that formula for life one more time as it is worth repeating.

Thoughts = Feelings = Actions = Results

Remember, if you want your results to change in your life, go back to your thoughts—change those!

"If you think you can or you think you can't, you are right." – Henry Ford

Understand the Impact Action Work

Think about what is going on in your career, in your relationships, in your health. Then write down the results that you have in your life now. For example:

Career
1. I am looking for another job
2. I like my job most days
3. I find it hard to go to work every day

Relationships
1. I find my coworkers annoying
2. My husband/wife just doesn't understand
3. I just wish my kids would pitch in more

Health
1. I am dieting right now
2. I need to lose weight
3. I am tired all the time

Review your thoughts on these results. Now write at least two *positive* thoughts around each result. Use this format:

Results	Current Thoughts	Defined Thoughts
Tired	I just wish I had more energy.	I wake up energized each day.
10 lbs.	I need to lose weight.	I love my body.
Job	I am just getting by in my job.	I love what I do and am empowered to do what I love.
Relationship	My husband/wife doesn't understand me.	I communicate my feelings clearly to others, which helps empower us.

It's important to begin noticing your thoughts as you have them—each and every moment. Paying attention to your thoughts means you can start to train your mind to make different choices on them. When life happens (and it will), you can begin to define your thoughts on creating your life.

Speaking of "life happens," one of the hardest things for us to do is to define the thoughts we have around these situations. If we make the choice to constantly and consistently *react* to what goes on in our everyday life, then we will continue to live in our unhappiness, our suffering in comfort. If we take responsibility for *our actions* and make a different choice (changing our thoughts instead of just the actions), then we begin to shift our awareness and our understanding—and our results. We feel lighter, more confident, more in the moment making decisions from our *defined* mind and not our reactionary mind.

When you become a "creator" in your life and not a "reactor," not only have you moved your "c," you've choosen to be free!

Take the Next Step

"The first step towards getting somewhere is to decide that you are not going to stay where you are." -John Pierpont Morgan

Take the Next Step – Tame Your Fear Through ROAR

Every action starts with a first step. Most of us are afraid to take that first step. And yet, it is with one step after another that we get where we want to be. Here's what can get us off the "dread center." We have to make a choice that *we want what is on the other side of fear.*

For me, my fear was moving beyond my grief. I was afraid that if I stopped grieving, then I would stop loving Al. I would forget him and our time together. It felt like a betrayal. It did not matter that he chose to leave me. All that mattered was for me not to forget him and the love we had together.

So, when the infamous phone call came in from my psychologist friend Phil, in his ever so "soft voice of understanding," my fear showed up as being pissed. How dare he even suggest that I forget about Al and move on with my life! That was blasphemy!

This is what happened next. Phil left a voice message for me. I can't remember whether or not I called him back. All I remember is that I was so angry with Phil that acknowledging his call was more than I could deal with at that time. Pain, pain, suffer, suffer.

Starting with Anger

That phone call made something in me snap. Before this, I was lethargic about everything going on around me. I was in a daze, just putting one foot in front of the other. You know what I mean. Sometimes I would lash out in anger at other people. My boss was one person who was on the other end of my anger. Now this is *never* a good thing! Again, I had "angels" watching over me.

Phil's call made me angry enough to start really looking at my thoughts and the results I was creating in my life. And I began to *feel* again. It was like I was waking up from being a zombie. I realized that this was no longer what I wanted—or at least not every hour of every day. Baby steps, away from this pain, were what I needed.

This spark of aliveness felt great. Yet it also brought up the much-dreaded four-letter word: **FEAR**. It's ironic, because that's where I was living most of the time anyway! Yet I didn't recognize that until I remembered a time that Al encouraged me through my fear.

Choosing Happiness Over Fear

It was a time in my life that I felt really unhappy in my job. I was working with a new financial publishing group. My experience of selling ad space into a monthly business newspaper prompted this company to recruit me. I was game, as it was something exciting to take on.

After about six months, it became clear that the company didn't realize the long selling cycle of financial institutions. They felt that within a month a bank would just say "yes" to putting out a monthly newspaper that was an advertising piece for their current and potential customers. Having just sold one bank on this new concept with others in the funnel, it was clear to all of us that it was not going to work. So, ironically, on the day I decided to resign, the company let me go.

I remember that day clearly, because I had just decided to get out of a job that made me unhappy. It was a mutual decision, to have the company let me go so I could draw unemployment. That *did* make me feel a bit of a failure. Yet, I was happier at that moment than I had been in a long time.

It took a few months to find another job, and it was a job that I was unsure would work for me. With Al's encouragement, I went into storefront retail, selling a new line of cleansing products. This was so different from anything I had ever done before. Here I was, a woman with a masters in counseling, and I was doing sample product cleansing demos and after store parties with women looking to keep their youthful appearance. That was what I thought before I took the job. Yet the potential for learning the business and running my own store was what I was really after, and was what helped to make this choice for myself.

Al's belief in me was what helped me to step through my fear of never having done anything like this—not quite knowing how to stop the negative voice inside my head of telling me I would fail. It was Al's voice and actions of support that were louder than the voice in my head. He gave me a card on my first day, on which he wrote, "You stepped out of your comfort zone into the darkness, to see the greatness beyond." I kept it with me all that day. And I still pull it out when I need it.

I tell you this story because I want *you* to step in to your darkness. I *promise* you, there is greatness beyond—if only you allow it!

Fear is the mechanism that allows us to grow if only we allow it.

Fear will always be with us. All we can do is choose how we allow it to define us. Do we let fear keep us stuck in our suffering? Or do we permit it to be with us and push us into greatness. This is the true question for you. It's the only one you need to answer.

Some of us think we should aim to become "fearless." In my opinion, that is impossible. Fear of something or someone will always be there. Choosing to ignore it doesn't mean we are fearless. It just means that we haven't faced the one thing that will bring us to our knees, gasping for breath, closing our eyes to shut out the thing that we FEAR the most. What we want to do is to learn how to tame our fear—to befriend our fear and make it our own.

Making a Friend of Fear

How do we make fear our friend? To have fear be with us and push us forward into our greatness? Let's first look at how fear shows up in our lives.

First, our fears are rarely what we think they are. Our perception of our fears are just *that*—a perception. Breaking it down into its biological aspect, we see that fear is a struggle in our brains between the thalamus and the frontal lobe. The thalamus—which is responsible for identifying physical and verbal risks and threats—produces our fear. The frontal lobe—which is responsible for our higher reasoning powers—makes our choices. Because it is all in our head and not real, *we are basically doing it to ourselves*—producing our fear for some reason. Why? Could it be out of a need to have fear in our life to make us feel alive?

Fear is defined as "an unpleasant emotion caused by the belief that someone or something is dangerous, likely to cause pain, or a threat."

All of us have had times when we experienced that definition of fear. A dog growled at us as a child, and we thought it would bite us. We were driving too fast down a dark highway and an animal came out of nowhere, causing us to swerve uncontrollably and not know how it would end. We were on vacation suddenly finding ourselves in a place we instinctively knew was not safe—where people are staring at us and making it clear that we do not belong! We have all been there: either through a real event or in our imagination.

Reality Check: How Real *Is* Your Fear?

Here's the interesting question. Was this "feeling" of fear that we had real—because we were *truly* in danger? Or was it a *perception* we held that caused us to experience this sense of fear?

How many times have you been held up at gunpoint and had your life threatened? How often have you been chased by a dangerous animal (a grizzly bear or a cougar)?

Or have we just experienced fear in our minds? Afraid that we will be the next ones laid off from our job as the company goes through financial difficulties. Afraid that the one we love is cheating on us. Afraid that we will lose everything that we have worked so hard for in our life and become "homeless."

Bag Lady Bound!

That was one of *my* biggest fears: that I was going to lose it all and end up on the streets as a homeless bag lady. When I was having this fear, it seemed as if it *could* really happen—as if it *would* happen the very next day. I am not sure where this idea came from, but I began acting like it was a very real possibility. I started to feel as if I had to hoard possessions, food, money. I had to be prepared to be in survival mode.

What I do know is when I was having this fear thought, I was extremely unhappy in my work, in my relationships, in my income, in almost every area of my life. Even though I really had no debt to speak of, was in a stable job, and was in a relationship at the time—

I still had the fear feeling of "losing" it all and being a bag lady! My imagination was defining my life and the choices I was making.

Here's what I learned from this experience. Most of the time, we make up the thoughts that scare us—the "what ifs" in our lives. What if I lose my job? What if I can't afford to pay my bills? What if my husband divorces me? We allow these scenarios to control us and our feelings. And along the way, we create an almost self-fulfilling prophecy that those things will happen.

How Fear Shows Up in Our Lives

Let's look at ways that fear can show up in our lives.

The most common form of fear dates back to prehistoric times: the fight, flight or freeze kind of fear. This was a time when everyday events could kill you if you didn't have the sense to be afraid, and the fight, flight or freeze technique to survive the situation. Remember the definition of fear: an unpleasant emotion caused by the *belief* that someone or something is dangerous, likely to cause pain, or a threat. Well, in those days, it was more than just a belief. It was a reality.

The most common form *now* is when it feels as if someone is holding you down and suffocating you—even when it is only just you and your mind doing this. You feel as if you will die as the life that you know is seeping out of you through this moment of fear.

Since the situation of being physically threatened is not common for most people, what other ways does fear appear for us?

It can be experienced as anxiety, doubt, worry—all of those types of words that begin to weigh us down. We identify all of these feelings as fear.

There is another way that fear can show up, which is a bit more seductive. This is a feeling of exhaustion, zoning out, or shutting down and just not dealing with something. That is a common way for fear to show up for us, and yet we don't know it as fear! How many times in your life were you so exhausted that you could barely get out of bed? Or you just zoned out and shut down: in front of the TV, mind numbingly doing nothing. This is what fear can look like for some people.

It appears as exhaustion because we can't even begin to deal with the emotional state that fear will put us in. We have learned to tune it out to avoid feeling the unpleasantness. Whatever is going on for us (financial problems, relationship problems, potential of losing a job, etc.), we choose to shut down instead.

How do we deal with—and not avoid—the fear that comes up in our lives? First, we need to understand that when we feel fear, it is an opportunity to grow. We are being asked or pushed to go beyond our comfort zone and to grow. This is a time of choice: to stay stuck or go beyond our suffering in comfort, so we can begin to live life on our own terms.

Use ROAR to Tame Your Fear

I have developed a four-step practice that will help you to tame your fear, called ROAR:

R – *Recognize* that fear is just a state of being in your life at this moment—and that it will not last forever. Our bodies aren't physically able to maintain this highly charged emotional state for long. Once we recognize our fear and how it shows up for us, we can move to the next step.

O – *Open up* to how your body has been conditioned to feel in fear. Are you feeling constricted, as though you're being choked or suffocated? Or just tired? Be open to these feelings and to the possibility of choosing to feel differently. You can decide to no longer view it as debilitating and limiting—choose to see and feel it as more powerful and enriching—because this is an opportunity for you.

A – *Accept* the new feeling that you now associate with fear. Fear is just that: an opportunity to step out of what we know now and into the unknown where beautiful things can happen. Breathe into this newness of growth, allowing your mind to catch up with your feelings. Own it and make it yours.

R – *Release* your old feelings, your old fear story and replace it with the new one. When you begin to feel the old story surfacing, immediately stop whatever it is that you are doing; literally hit your internal pause button. Say out loud or to yourself, "This is no longer me. I choose to move out of my comfort into something *more*."

This practice of **ROAR** is commonly called a "pattern-interrupt process": a behavioral shift. We begin to notice the pattern that has been our story for so long and literally choose a different one.

Our thoughts, our memories and our stories have an attachment to us—our stories become our memories. Good and bad memories latch on to us as muscle memory. We tend to only remember the bad (failures) muscle memories, including those created by fearful moments in our lives. Whatever story we had in the past has literally become part of our bodies and made us who we are. This then creates our thoughts. When we begin to recognize our thoughts, we have the power to ask, "Is it really me?"

A pain, a hurt, a loneliness ... But we also have memories of successes: getting the "A" on a test when you didn't think it was possible or winning an award or million dollar project. Remembering the successes in our lives—this muscle memory of *success* from our past—is what we need to put first in our being. We must invite these success memories to replace the less empowering thoughts: the memory of failure. We *have* our story, but we *are not* our story. We have our memories, but we are not our memories.

How do we nurture our faith in all that we want to do, to be, to create when fear comes into our life? First we recognize that fear will always be with us. It is not something that will just go away because we now know about it. Yet, we now have a choice of what we want to do with it. We can choose to have fear pull us down and never be able to move forward with our life. Or we can use our fear to push us forward by allowing it to become our friend. Our friend because we can choose to change our feelings toward it—which changes our actions and results.

Work toward reframing your thoughts on fear!

"Forget safety.

Live where you fear to live.

Destroy your reputation.

Be notorious."

– Rumi

Take the Next Step Action Work

Make a list of all your fears. Write down every situation that, when you think about it, it causes you to panic or shut down. This should include fearful thoughts or situations that *have* happened to you, or things you are afraid *might* happen.

Let's work on the process of re-patterning.

Spend some time on this exercise. Set aside a block of uninterrupted time for your reframing and re-patterning work.

Look at your first fear. Breathe in to it. Relax your body and your mind. Name the feeling you associate with this fear and write it down. Do this for every fearful item on your list. You will probably begin to see a pattern in the list of fears.

Now for each fear ask yourself this question, "Is this *really true* in my life, or is it just my perception of something that *could* be?" Take time and be truthful in your answers.

Feel how freeing this can be when you realize that these situations are just that, *thoughts,* and not something life threatening that could happen to you.

Once we realize this and do our work with **ROAR**, we can begin to experience fear as a friend, pushing us forward and not holding us back.

How does your fear show up in your life?

How to Tame Your Fear in 4 Steps:
R O A R

R   Recognize that fear is just a state of being in your life at this moment. It is not defining you forever.

O   Open up to the feelings that you have been conditioned to feel - open up to the possibility of being able to make a different choice of how you feel, no longer seeing fear as debilitating, limiting, but seeing and feeling it as powerful and enriching.

A   Accept the new feeling that you now associate with fear. Breathe into this newness allowing your mind to catch up with your feelings. Own it — make it yours!

R   Release your old fear story and replace it with your new story. When you begin to feel the old story surfacing, hit the pause button and say, "That used to be me. I am now…"

www.denisehansard.com

Step into Greatness

"The world won't step into its Greatness until we step into ours." -Marianne Williamson

Step into Greatness – Own Your Choices

When you choose to do this work, you invest in yourself to become more! Then you can know this in your heart. You will not go to your grave regretting having done certain things or not having done others. Not having told people you loved them. Not feeling the love of others. Not living every day successfully. And not being the happiest that you could ever be.

We always have choices. There are many times we may feel as if all of our choices have been taken away. This is not true. We can always choose how we invest in ourselves through our thoughts, our feelings and our actions.

When I was working through my grief, choosing to receive professional help, I invested in the *me* I am today. I was initially making the choice to stay "stuck," to stay comfortable in my pain. Remember my mantra: "pain, pain, suffer, suffer"? This was where I lived. And I lived there way too long.

My years of choosing to stay "somewhat" stuck were the only choice I felt I had. Days and weeks would go by where I was *good*. I felt that I had gotten through the worst part of the grief and could begin to live my life again. Then the pain would hit me all at once, striking when I least expected it. I was blindsided with the impact of it all. It was as if that eventful day, when I found Al in his garage—looking like he was just asleep, resting peacefully—was happening all over again. The panic I felt when, at first, all I found was the *note*. The frantic search to find him—deep inside hoping I was wrong: that he would not be dead. The moment I did find him, trying to decide whom to call first. All of those feelings, reliving it all again and again, would sneak up on me.

Then there were moments that I was healing and I was taking steps toward being me again. Yet, I unconsciously would do things that showed I still believed suicide *might* still be a potential choice for me.

"Are You Planning on *Killing* Yourself?"

One such time was when my friend and I went to visit my younger sister. We had tons of fun with her and my nephew: going to the aquarium, laughing and playing. When I was leaving, I gave my sister my pearl necklace. This took her totally off guard. I vividly remember the look on her face—shock, concern and love. Very bluntly, she looked me in the eye and asked, "Are you planning on killing yourself?" Now was my turn to be shocked. This thought didn't cross my mind when I *made* the decision to give her the necklace. I was not over my grief, my pain … I was still trying to find ways to heal. I didn't realize until that moment that I was acting just like a person who could kill herself—who could take her life, just like Al did.

I made the choice then and there to begin working harder to get past my pain. My decision to give my sister the necklace was due to my feelings toward possessions at that time. Possessions felt *heavy*. They were just items and not worth a lot to me, especially this necklace. I thought this piece of jewelry looked so much like my sister that I couldn't think of anyone else wearing it. To this day, it was the right choice—because she wears it all the time. I realized that I wanted to show the people I loved that I loved them; probably more than I loved myself at that time. Even though giving away possessions is a sign of letting go of oneself, to me, it was OK to express my love in any way that I could. Giving her that necklace was one of those ways.

This was the moment I chose to go beyond my comfort into the great unknown: investing in the "me" that was worth being whole, without being tied to my victimhood of suicide. This process was the hardest work I've done in my life. But I stuck with this choice—no matter how difficult it felt at times. There was no turning back. My life depended on it.

Transformation or Not ... Here I Come

This process of transformation, of becoming a new me, took years. During this time, I often felt as though with every few steps forward, I took at least as many steps back. I persisted, because "pain, pain, suffer, suffer" was no longer a choice for me. Feeling trapped in the old story of what had defined me so far had become a very uncomfortable place—and I wasn't going to stay there anymore. I choose to live!

Does this sound familiar? Are you feeling trapped by your choices? Money may be an issue for you. Depression could be weighing on you because of an unhappy job situation, or a relationship you may or may not have. You may be experiencing that trapped feeling: of drowning in three feet of water, with no idea on what to do. The thought of standing up just hasn't seemed possible.

When you're here, it's time to begin stepping into greatness by investing in a new you and owning the choices you make in everyday life. If it feels as though life is dealing you a bad hand, just realize that you hold the cards. You hold the cards on what you think about, on what you choose to feel, and on how you are going to deal with those thoughts and feelings.

Remember the quote hanging in my office that helps me every day:

"It is not what happens to you, but what you do with what happens to you that matters."

This can now become a part of your everyday life, too. Once we can notice our thoughts, and choose the ones that define rather than destroy us, we have the key. This key prevents us from being our own jailer. Everything we do in life is by choice, and now you can feel free to choose. Even in the direst situations, you may choose to have thoughts that bring peace and happiness. By owning the choice of how you think, you can set yourself free. You can break free from the jail that you previously choose to be in.

Everything in life is a choice. Owning your choices set you free!

How do we use these choices to move into our greatness? It's simple. Recognize that *everything* is *always* a choice. We have to stop pretending this isn't true. That's what we do every time we say things like this:

"I'm just not sure."
"I can't make a decision right now."
"I need more information before I can choose."
"I don't know."

These statements are *all* choices. But we often use them and pretend they're not. Every time these words leave our lips, what we're really saying is "no." Yet we use those phrases because we're afraid an outright "no" means we'll miss an opportunity. And if we *do*, then we can blame circumstances, the environment, whatever. Because if we came out and said "no," we would have to hold ourselves accountable for what happens in our lives.

When you feel as if you have no choice in life, you become victimized. You're stuck in quicksand and not able to move forward. When you begin to own your choices, you free yourself. Here's how you do this.

Steps Toward Freedom

Recognition is the first step. You recognize the words you use every day help to define your story. Are you *"better"* or *"bitter"*? Are you a *"victor"* or a *"victim"*? Watch how these simple words can cause us to shrink or to expand. Words are powerful. They hold a charge; an electricity. Our use of words and phrases will determine our feelings of being stuck or of being free—to live as we were meant to live.

Imagination is the second step. When we were young, we were constantly asked, "What do you want to be when you grow up?" We had the greatest of imaginations then! Our answers were an astronaut, a policeman, a lion tamer, a ballerina, or just about anything we could think of in that moment. The power to use *our thoughts* to create *our reality* through *our words* became one of our greatest treasures. We *still* have this power. We can use it to visualize greatness: to do things we didn't think were possible. To endure the toughest moments in our lives. And to create our dreams of what we would love. To me, Walt Disney has the best description of this: "If you can dream it, you can do it."

Choice is the final step. The words we choose can either empower us or keep us stuck. Here are some of the biggest dream-blocking words we can use:

I can't ...
I have to ...
Whatever (infused with great sarcasm)
I don't know
I want to, **but** *...*
How can I?

Each of these phrases has a feeling attached to it—and most of these feelings aren't "good": giving up, being stuck, or just plain and simple frustration.

When you are having money issues, the most common phrase you use is "I can't," as in "I can't do that because I don't have the money." When your relationship is not going well, "whatever" or "I don't know" pop up continuously: "Whatever you say is *fine*." or "I don't know! What do you want me to do, or to say?" On the job, you find yourself constantly repeating "how" as in "How am I supposed to get that done when I am not sure what I am supposed to be doing?" or "I want to, but" as in "I want to, but I don't have the time or resources." Maybe you say these things because you're not sure where you stand in the organization and feel a bit like an outcast.

When we own our choices, we hold ourselves accountable.

So make a choice and own it. A dear friend and boss once told me that the most powerful thing I could do in life: "Make a choice and follow through on that choice. As long as it doesn't kill anyone, you are doing the best thing you can do." What great advice! He knew I was still healing and that was what I needed to hear the most. Because, at that time, I would sometimes begin to waffle about any decision—*period*. Should I or shouldn't I? Could I or couldn't I? – When this happened, I would freeze: be unable to make the simplest of choices, much less business choices. Take the advice that I got: "Don't waffle and second-guess your way through life."

Make choices. And make them the most empowering ones you can in that moment. You can always change them later if it turns out that this wasn't really what you wanted. It is less about what choice you *make* and more about *making* a choice! Begin creating energy around you by just making a choice and then owning it.

The words we use can help us live into being confident. We suddenly have our "Mojo," "our groove" back. We become the person who gets the next position in the organization, the person everyone wants to be around, or the person who has all the luck.

One More Story …

My last corporate job was one where, from my very first day, I knew it was not going to work out. After having spent 16 years in the corporate world being an expert in the field of pricing, I could immediately see the writing on the wall that this new position would not last. The question really became, "How long will it last?"

It took only eight months for the company to realize that they did not have the fortitude to have a Pricing Department that meant something. The day my boss came in to tell me that the department was being dissolved, and many people were being let go in a RIF (reduction in force), I was relieved. For so long, I had been living out of alignment with what I knew the Pricing Department could be. I was caught in the middle of a corporate fight between the "sales" view of life and the "finance" view of life. This was not the life I wanted for me.

So, when my boss told me the news, I made a choice on my reaction to this. The words I chose and spoke were clear: "Thank you. This is a blessing in disguise." Needless to say, these were not the words he was expecting. His was prepared for tears and anger and having to find a way to excuse himself without harm. With the words I spoke, he was shocked and had no idea how to deal with my defined choice.

Right before I left the company, he let me how pleased he was with my professionalism in handling the situation. He thanked me. He had never had anyone to do what I had done—take my life into my own hands with my choices ... defining my freedom in a difficult situation.

Choosing and owning the choices we make is how we get to the final step of our new, great life: the life you were meant to live. Join me there!

"Every choice in life has its own unique and inherent challenges and will bring about change ..." -InspirationalThinkTank.com

Step into Your Greatness Action Work

This exercise is all about you and who you want to become in this process. Being able to make choices and own those choices: that's the real work and ultimate reward.

Let's begin!

Make a conscious choice to notice the words you use every day. Not just speaking and writing them, but *thinking* them.

Keep a running list of these words. Fill up your journal with pages of them. Yes, there will be pages. You are speaking, writing, or thinking more *un-empowering* words than you know.

Once you have this list, think of better words you can use instead Here are some examples:

Current Choice	More Empowering Choice
I can't	I choose
I have to	I prefer
How	What is one thing
Why	Why not
Coulda, shoulda, woulda	Choose, choose, choose

Now is the moment of truth for you. *Can you decide to make different choices on your words?*

When you begin to notice what you are thinking, you will shift into a different perspective of being. You will choose to think differently, to speak differently and to act differently. This is the process of transformation. Tune into awareness. Tame fear through ROAR. And tap into your greatness. You have the power!

Your words are powerful!
Choose them wisely.

What Do You Do Now?

"You cannot change your destination overnight, but you can change your direction overnight." -Jim Rohm

Breathe, just breathe! This has been a journey for all of us. Congratulations for diving into this work and making choices to set yourself FREE!

Here is what you did during this work:

- You opened up to your story by becoming aware. Now you know that your story doesn't define you, nor does it control your future.
- You started understanding the impact your choices have on your life. Now you know that to change your results, you must begin with your thoughts.
- You tamed your fear through ROAR:
    o Recognize
    o Open up
    o Accept
    o Release and replace

    Now you know that you actually can make fear your friend and turn it from a negative feeling of avoidance into one that signals an opportunity to grow.
- You stepped into your greatness by finding your Mojo! Now you know that the most important action you can

take is to make a choice and then own it—or change it to a better one.

The Rest of Your *Life*!

This is the work of your life. If you do it, you will transform yourself. And this won't only happen in your personal life. The results from this work are just as powerful in your professional world. What better gift to give yourself than to be free to make choices in how you define the work that you do, with whom you do it, and how it will be in the long run.

Think about this. One key to being a great leader is to make choices, own those choices, and then to communicate those choices to those around you. It's up to you to take control of your thoughts and ultimately your results, so you and everyone in the company can be the *best* that all of you were meant to be.

We know that everything can and will change. We have had it happen in our lives and seen it in other people's. The question becomes how you want to deal with the changes that come about in *your* life.

Be honest with yourself. Do you choose to say goodbye to everything that is familiar to you, which is comfortable even in its pain? Can you cut the cord to that old story that no longer serves you—on your way to a new you?

The Time to Make a Choice is Now

Stepping into change is a choice. Yet, suffering in the comfort of our pain is also a choice. Own which choice you *really* want in your life.

Here's the truth. When you change, some people will leave you and endings will happen. Just as true, however, is some things will never change. The essence of who you really are deep down will remain the same. It will just evolve into a greater and better you!

This is what I do in my business, in my speaking engagements and for my clients. I take them through the steps they need to transform their lives. I offer them the support to bring about that transformation and give them the tools to do this again and again on their own.

Here are some of the results I've been honored to see:

- People become gainfully employed after being out of work for almost a year. They find the confidence to go after what they truly want in their career and have the clarity to define the activities needed to get there.
- Couples save their long-term relationship so they can get back to the *"in-love"* stage they once embraced and honored.
- People stop sabotaging the good work they put into their current companies or are able to start new ones.
- People gain confidence, clarity and intention toward defining the life they are meant to live.
- People feel empowered to take that next step into their own greatness. After a seminar, they tell me, "You were talking directly to me!"

If you're wondering, "What Do I Do Now?" You have several choices:

- You can put the book on the shelf and be happy that you read it or not, but not really change anything in your life. This is a *choice*—own that choice and stop the blame game.

- You can re-read this book and really put your *whole* self into the exercises. Choose to make the needed changes for you to become more empowered.
- You can go to my website (www.denisehansard.com) sign up to receive my blogs and other cool stuff, so you can stay in the practice.

The best thing you can do now is to make a choice. A choice for the next step in your life toward a new you.

Making a choice to be free is the greatest gift you can give yourself. Let's take the journey together.

If you would love to take your next step but are not quite sure how to go about that, allow me to help. If you are serious about working toward a new you, go to my website and sign up for a complimentary *Exhausted to Exhilarated* Discovery Session. This will allow us to really look at what you would love in your life and discuss what you feel has stopped you so far. We will work together to determine what a good next step can be for you. This session is valued at $250—which you will receive for *free* because you bought this book. Sign up, make the choice to follow through, and move toward your greatness!

www.denisehansard.com

"Let Your Greatness Blossom."

– Nelson Mandela

Why Not?

"This life is what you make it. No matter what, you're going to mess up sometimes, it's a universal truth. But the good part is you get to decide how you're going to mess it up. Girls will be your friends—they'll act like it anyway. But just remember, some come, some go. The ones that stay with you through everything—they're your true best friends. Don't let go of them. Also remember, sisters make the best friends in the world. As for lovers, well, they'll come and go too. And baby, I hate to say it, most of them—actually pretty much all of them are going to break your heart, but you can't give up because if you give up, you'll never find your soul mate. You'll never find that half who makes you whole and that goes for everything. Just because you fail once, doesn't mean you're gonna fail at everything. Keep trying, hold on, and always, always, always believe in yourself, because if you don't, then who will, sweetie? So keep your head high, keep your chin up, and most importantly, keep smiling, because life's a beautiful thing and there's so much to smile about." -Marilyn Monroe

Life is what you make it through your choices. In the continued work on myself, I have learned to love myself and others; I have learned to trust me and the process; I have made choices toward defining my life in every moment.

Peaceful Eye or Swirling Tornado?

There was a time when little things would throw me into a tailspin keeping me swirling and out of control. These times could last for months. I would stay "stuck" in my depression, questioning everything that I did, doing the same thing over and over again with no difference.

As I began this work on me, as it is outlined in this book, I suddenly noticed that I would need to make different choices. And when I did this, my "stuckness" didn't last as long. Suddenly it was only days that I was stuck. And then it became hours. Then minutes. And now it has become seconds—when I recognize my "stuckness" and make a different choice. I can quickly move out of what I don't want through the simple process of recognizing the choices I have in my thoughts creating my results.

My thoughts or my "stuckness" would show up as sadness, confusion, overwhelm, and just plain tired. I know this is how it shows up for some of you. I can hear the very words that went through my head and may be going through yours:

"Why can't I be the one?"
"Why am I so invisible?"
"Why can't I get the promotion?"
"Why, why, why?"

As I evolved through this process, I became like Eeyore from the Winnie the Pooh books, whose penchant for doom and gloom became his outlook on life.

"Wish I could say yes, but I can't."

Yet, he had moments of wisdom even in a depressed way of being.

"It's not much of a tail, but I'm sort of attached to it."

Eeyore was me or I was Eeyore.

His approach to acceptance is the way most people go about living their life ... just barely acknowledging that they can have more.

A Child's Tale ...

When I was ten years old, I played softball. I am a tomboy at heart and playing was fun! Here was a game where I was more than good—I was great!

Imagine a hot summer afternoon in June in the south. The sun is shining and there are 10 girls on a softball field, manning every position, with an umpire behind the plate and a girl up to bat. The bases were loaded and the girl up to bat is me! The ball is pitched. "Strike one!" the ump calls. The next pitch comes and is called a ball outside. Then the third pitch comes and I swing as hard as I can—sending that ball flying to the outfield and over the fence. I hit a GRAND SLAM homerun! What an experience! I am congratulated by all my teammates as I run into the dugout after jumping on home plate. I'm excited for myself and yet don't want to show this excitement. And I also have the feeling that this was my job, my reason for playing—get all the other players to score runs.

A couple of innings go by. My team now is out in the field. I am playing the shortstop position that rotates between third and second base. The opposing team is up to bat. There are girls on first and second bases. The girl at bat hits a fly ball—right at me. I catch the fly ball! The girl on second runs to third and is tagged out ... by me. The girl on first runs for second, not knowing I had caught the fly ball. And tag: she is out. I had just made a triple play without moving more than two feet from where I caught the fly ball.

No one is aware that this was a triple out. Even the umpire calls it a double. Then I hear my mother yelling and crying out that her daughter had made a triple out all by herself. She is so proud of me! Then everyone else realizes the same thing. In this moment, all the cheers are for *me*. The patting on the back with "Way to go!" are all for me! It is too much for this little girl with *not good enough* feelings to take. I run to the dugout and start crying. This game with all its greatness is just too overwhelming to accept into my life.

Where I am Today

I have come a long way from that day. Just the other day, my mom told me that people talked for years about that one game and that one girl who hit the Grand Slam homerun and made the triple out. Every time, she proudly boasted that that was her daughter!

Here is where I am going to boast proudly of my work and with what other people say about it. I am going to own the choices I have made in being a Transformational Life Coach with pricing expertise and a Professional Speaker.

This is what my clients say:

> *Denise has guided me through the process of aligning my dreams, skills, and needs to discover my life purpose. She*

has helped me to get my dreams and vision down on paper, revise them as needed as I continue to learn and grow, and take the action needed to achieve them. Denise has provided me caring, compassionate guidance that I could not get from reading a self-help book. She has showed me how to tackle the fears that prevent me from achieving my life goals by taking action. As she promised when I started working with her, Denise has remained determined to make sure I progress toward my dreams. She has never given up on me.
Joan Van Allen

Working with Denise has been a tremendous experience. Coaching sessions with her never feel clinical or like an obligation. She is truly gifted with guiding and coaching you to focus your vision so that you can fulfill your dream.
B.J. Phillips

Denise Hansard is a "hands-on" coach. She gives you tools to make meaningful and lasting changes in your life and business. Her step-by-step approach, customized to every student's needs, is easy to follow. If you are serious in making progress in life, Denise is the coach who will take you to the NEXT level. She did that for me!
Marzena M. Melby

One of Denise's gifts is her calm but energizing voice. You'll hear it in this book, sharing her wisdom and encouraging you to make choices that will serve you.
Lynne Franklin

Although I had worked with several business coaches, it

wasn't until I worked with Denise that I was able to define my dreams and goals from the heart out, identify and overcome the obstacles that held me in the way of my own success, and empower me with the belief in the limitless possibilities life has to offer. I have remembered to believe in myself again, and I am having a really good time while I live and work more fully. And it's contagious!
Leah Richter

Here is what others who know me have said:

I interviewed Denise for an expert call for my Strategic Success Club. The call was great, and she gave us a lot of wonderful information we could implement right away. Denise knows what she's talking about!
Tara Truax
Author, Who the Hell Am I to Start a Business?

Denise recently gave a presentation to job search candidates. She was able to resonate with the variety of individuals using an engaging and consultative approach. Denise's presentation was both intellectually stimulating and applicable to the transition process and larger goal setting. She gave realistic tips without overwhelming and coached them to make the right decisions for their own paths. The session was more like a conversation between friends than a presentation.
Michelle Tasevski
Right Management

"Denise offered her time and expertise to a business networking group I organized. She helped everyone understand the concept of achieving one's goals. Denise

used a group exercise to help each of us identify a fear or doubt that is stopping me from pursuing a goal or dream. The outcome was very beneficial and gave everyone some ideas on how to overcome our thoughts that hold us back. The presentation was enjoyable and very helpful."
Mark Kardon

These words inspire me to continue growing; continue seeking out the needed experts for me to become more. Choose to do the same! Here's to a New You!

*"Be not afraid of greatness.
Some are born great, some achieve greatness,
and others have greatness thrust upon them."*

— William Shakespeare, Twelfth Night

"You were born with potential.

You were born with goodness and trust. You were born with ideals and dreams. You were born with greatness.

You were born with wings.

You are not meant for crawling, so don't.

You have wings.

Learn to use them and fly."

— Rumi

"In three words I can sum up everything I've learned about life: it goes on."

— *Robert Frost*

"Always be a first rate version of yourself and not a second rate version of someone else."

— *Judy Garland*

Live like you were meant to ...

"There is nothing wrong with your life. You have a 'good' job, a 'good' relationship, 'good' health, etc. But you know the enemy of 'great' is 'good.' Wouldn't you love to be GREAT! That's what I do for my clients. We work together to create the willingness to step into the transformational process of greatness!'

Denise started her career as a pricing expert, helping multi-million dollar corporations reach their revenue goals through the art and science of pricing. She was instrumental in training and coaching executives, sales teams, and others in understanding the dynamics of pricing and the power it could bring. With a master's degree in counseling from University of Georgia, one of Denise's desires was to help and serve others.

In 2012, she chose to follow her vision of a new life, by becoming a Certified Transformational Life Coach. Denise is a natural teacher and effective coach. She has been called a person who "has a passion for people, helping them realize their potential." Her teaching techniques through coaching or speaking offer a fun, inspiring methodology for helping individuals and groups move past what it is that is keeping them stuck into greatness in their life!

As a sought-after transformational life coach with pricing expertise and professional speaker, Denise offers inspiring talks and workshops to sold-out audiences around the country, as well as transformational in-depth coaching programs that help clients achieve new heights of success, meaning, and spiritual aliveness.

This is her commitment and her passion: helping others to live the life they would love! Whether it is to enhance your financial freedom, relationships with others, your health, or your vocation and career: isn't it better to have a partner who can help you reach those goals, those visions to step into Greatness?

Live the life you were meant to live.
Contact Denise to get started.

www.denisehansard.com
denise@denisehansard.com
https://facebook.com/coaching2dream

How to Tame Your Fear in 4 Steps:
R O A R

R — Recognize that fear is just a state of being in your life at this moment. It is not defining you forever.

O — Open up to the feelings that you have been conditioned to feel - open up to the possibility of being able to make a different choice of how you feel, no longer seeing fear as debilitating, limiting, but seeing and feeling it as powerful and enriching.

A — Accept the new feeling that you now associate with fear. Breathe into this newness allowing your mind to catch up with your feelings. Own it -- make it yours!

R — Release your old fear story and replace it with your new story. When you begin to feel the old story surfacing, hit the pause button and say, "That used to be me. I am now..."

www.denisehansard.com

Made in the USA
Middletown, DE
25 September 2015